PEGASUS PAPERBACK

© Copyright 2021
Zara Ahmed

The right of Zara Ahmed to be identified as author of
this work has been asserted by her in accordance with the
Copyright, Designs and Patents Act 1988.

All Rights Reserved

No reproduction, copy or transmission of this publication
may be made without written permission.

No paragraph of this publication may be reproduced,
copied or transmitted save with the written permission of the publisher, or in accordance
with the provisions
of the Copyright Act 1956 (as amended).

Any person who commits any unauthorised act in relation to
this publication may be liable to criminal
prosecution and civil claims for damages.

A CIP catalogue record for this title is
available from the British Library.
ISBN 978-1-91090-362-9

Pegasus is an imprint of
Pegasus Elliot MacKenzie Publishers Ltd.
www.pegasuspublishers.com

First Published in 2021

Pegasus
Sheraton House Castle Park
Cambridge England

Printed & Bound in Great Britain

the memory thief
by Zara Ahmed

Pegasus

Real life short stories from people who know someone with dementia, or are caring for someone with dementia.

WITH SPECIAL THANKS TO:
Eve, Maria, Ryan, Nosheen, khan, Marc, Amina, Beth, Matt, Sophie, Shan, John, Mack, and Jay.
Thank you for offering your wonderful stories.

what to expect

WHAT IS DEMENTIA?
True anecdotes from a variety of people of all genders, ages and ethnicities showing us the true depth of dementia.

DETAILS
Details about dementia that are not heard of a lot and are often left unexplained.

THE FUNNY SIDE
Looking at it from a lighter, slightly more positive way.

ADVICE
Advice ranging from personal experience to advice from professional carers of dementia patients.

What is Dementia

WHAT THE NHS SAYS:

Dementia is a blanket term for diseases and conditions characterized by a decline in memory, language, problem-solving and other thinking skills that affect a person's capability to perform everyday activities. Memory loss is an example. Alzheimer's is the most common cause of dementia.

Dementia is not a single disease; it's an overall term—like heart disease—that covers a wide range of specific medical conditions, including Alzheimer's disease. Disorders grouped under the general term 'dementia' are caused by abnormal brain changes. These changes trigger a decline in cognitive abilities, severe enough to impact and impair daily life and independent function. They also affect behaviour, feelings and relationships.

"My granddad had dementia and Alzheimer's and on multiple occasions he would un-wire himself and run to the pub. No one would know where he was and he was in the pub!" - Eve

8 What is Dementia

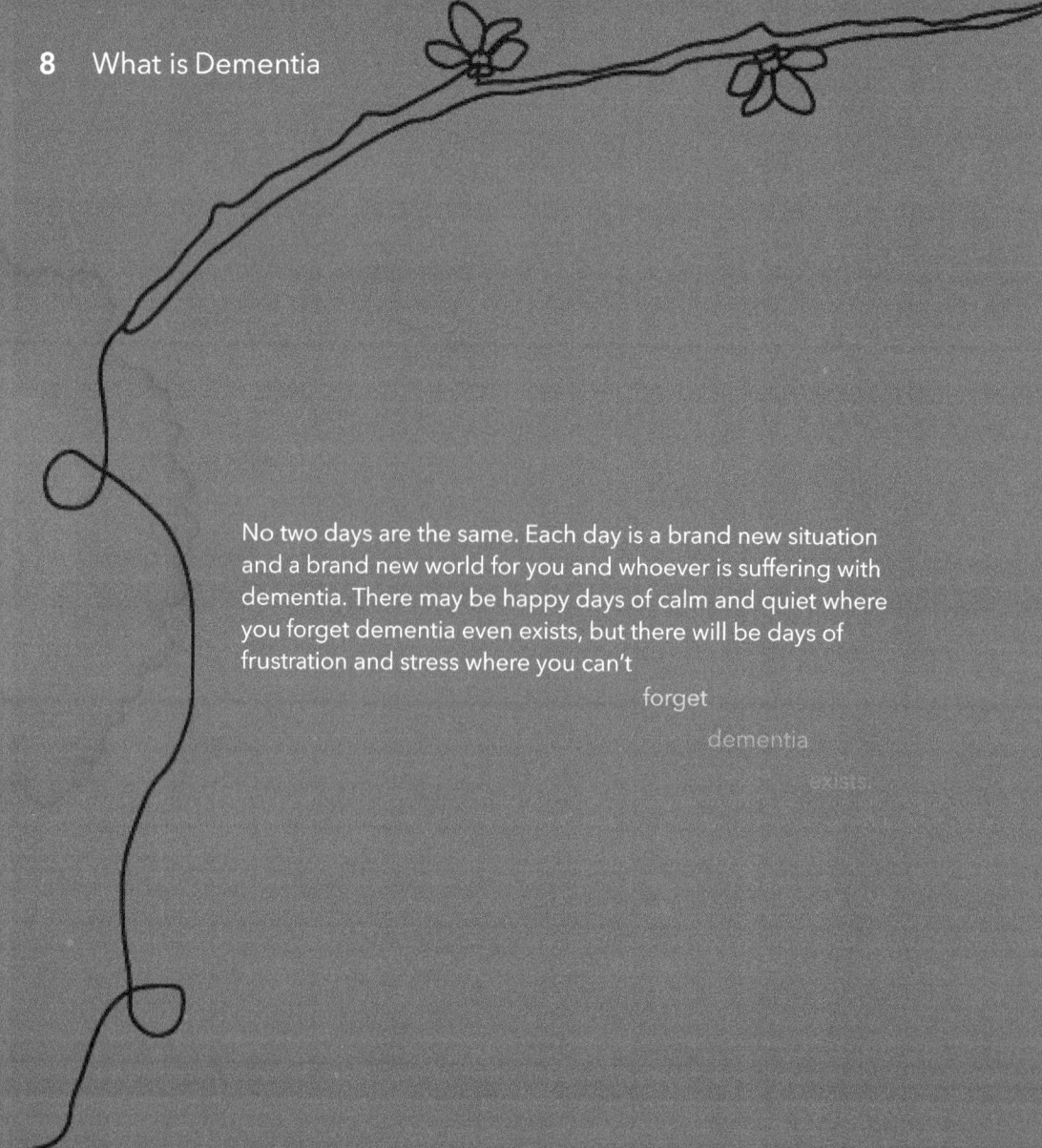

No two days are the same. Each day is a brand new situation and a brand new world for you and whoever is suffering with dementia. There may be happy days of calm and quiet where you forget dementia even exists, but there will be days of frustration and stress where you can't

forget

dementia

exists.

"MY JAPANESE GRANDMOTHER HAS DEMENTIA AND SHE FORGOT WHO I WAS LAST TIME I SAW HER THIS CHRISTMAS. SHE SAID, 'OH, A GAIJIN LADY!' (FOREIGNER) AS SOON AS SHE SAW ME." – Maria

Sometimes my father thinks someone has stolen his shoes. He will say these are not his shoes and that his actual shoes have been stolen by a thief." - Ryan

What is Dementia 11

SUSPICIONS:

Due to not being able to recognise their surroundings and the people around them, people with dementia can sometimes suspect their friends and family of stealing from them, among other things. This is due to the mistrust which is natural against strangers, and as they progress in their illness they may regard you as such, therefore making them wary and suspicious.

Showing them whatever they think has been stolen often solves this. However, sometimes they may not recognise the object as theirs, so the best thing to do is to distract them and try to take their minds off it. This can be hard, and sometimes it is best to just let someone else talk to them if they are suspecting you, or are angry with you.

"My mother-in-law calls me Trevor from the Navy. She doesn't even know anybody called Trevor who is in the Navy, so we can't work out where that came from!" – Marc

What is Dementia   **13**

REALITY:
Using different names for people they care about is often done when they have forgotten who you are or what your name is but still remember that there is some form of attachment, so they will give you someone else's name. This could be someone they know, or someone they saw in a film or read about in a book. Mixing up reality and fiction is a common trait amongst patients with dementia, so they may not be able to separate what is real and what isn't, which leaves them confused, and causes mixed up names and personalities.

"At three a.m. one night my gran woke up and demanded breakfast. We tried telling her it was the middle of the night but she refused to believe it, despite it still being dark outside!" – Zara

details

CLOCKS:

Testing dementia is not a linear process and it is a difficult illness to monitor, however, one way a GP can tell if an individual has dementia is asking them to draw a clock from memory with no assistance or time limit. These clocks drawn by dementia patients are often very strange and warped versions of a normal clock.

TIME:

Time is a funny thing with dementia; on top of generally not being able to tell the time from a clock, some of the more severe cases of dementia leave an individual unable to differentiate between night and day. Sometimes my gran will look at the dark night and tell me it's the middle of the day and vice versa. This is most likely due to the fact that they forget what day and night looks like, and what the light/dark represents.

"MY GREAT AUNT HAS EARLY ONSET DEMENTIA AND SOMETIMES THINKS SHE CAN SEE HER RELATIVES AND FRIENDS SITTING WITH HER." – Nosheen

Details **17**

YOU:
Sometimes caring for someone with dementia can be funny, sad, frustrating and exhausting. Especially when the dementia is particularly bad and the sufferer hallucinates or hears things, it can lead to them becoming angry which, in turn, can be frustrating for you. These are all normal, healthy responses and are nothing to feel guilty about.

HALLUCINATIONS:
Some individuals with dementia tend to hallucinate. They will hallucinate anything ranging from people such as relatives and friends, to animals and sounds. These hallucinations can sometimes have them saying some of the most bizarre things you'll ever hear. The best thing to do when someone is hallucinating is to either distract them or just agree with them. Telling them what they can see isn't real will just upset and frustrate them.

"She looked at the mirror and smiled. 'Who are you?' she asked. 'Come with me,' she insisted. My gran spent ages talking to her reflection as if she had met an old friend. Sometimes it was positive and sometimes she would get angry." - Zara

Details   **19**

REFLECTIONS:
Individuals with dementia tend not to understand mirrors; they seem to never recognise themselves, which sometimes leads to aggravation or, like the story opposite, someone to talk too. This could be due to them being unable to recognise people which would include themselves too. So, when they see someone they perhaps have not seen in a long time standing so close, they might get startled.

FIXATIONS:

People with dementia will often find something to fixate on. That could be anything and anyone. This will be something they will remember regularly, day in, day out, and even get agitated and upset if anyone tries to oppose or deny them this fixation. The best thing to do is to let it play out and just try and distract them if they have fixated on something that makes them frustrated and sad. This can be quite frustrating for the carer, as the fixation could be a person and they will then disregard everyone else in comparison to this certain individual. Instead of getting upset, the best thing to remember is they cannot control it, and it does not mean they love you any less. It's just their brain switching from either unfocused to very intensely focused on one particular subject.

"My gran fixates on one person sometimes and will revolve her entire day around asking and worrying if there is food for them, if they've eaten. She repeats herself for days." – Zara

"She looks at the TV and says, 'They can see me'. She thinks that the people in the TV know her and sometimes suspects they are talking about her." – Amina

Details 23

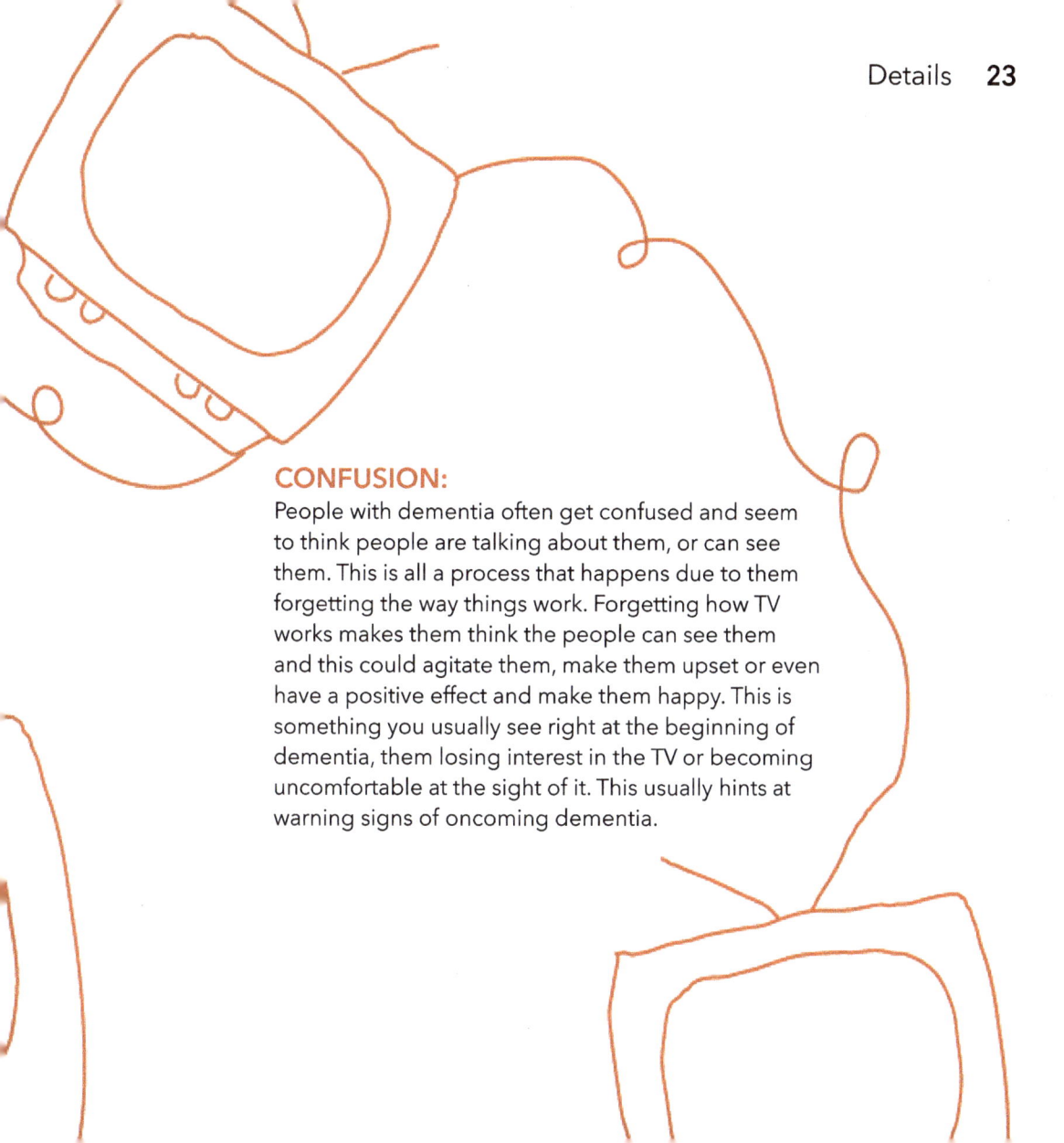

CONFUSION:
People with dementia often get confused and seem to think people are talking about them, or can see them. This is all a process that happens due to them forgetting the way things work. Forgetting how TV works makes them think the people can see them and this could agitate them, make them upset or even have a positive effect and make them happy. This is something you usually see right at the beginning of dementia, them losing interest in the TV or becoming uncomfortable at the sight of it. This usually hints at warning signs of oncoming dementia.

"MY GREAT AUNT HAS FORGOTTEN EVERYONE'S NAMES AND ONLY REMEMBERS THE NAME OF HER DAUGHTER, SO SHE CALLS US ALL BY HER DAUGHTER'S NAME." — **Nosheen**

NAMES:
One of the more common aspects of dementia that are well known is the forgetting of names. This is something that usually happens in the earlier stages and then progresses further as the disease develops. Sometimes a certain name may get stuck in their minds and they end up using it for many different people. This usually is a name of someone they hold dear as they remember the name due to its strong emotional attachment; they may not even remember who it belongs too, just that it is someone special.

"MY MOTHER OFTEN TALKS AS IF SHE IS YOUNG AGAIN. YOU CAN TELL SHE FORGETS HER REAL AGE AND RELAPSES IN TIME TO THIRTY/FORTY YEARS BACK." – Khan

TIME TRAVEL:

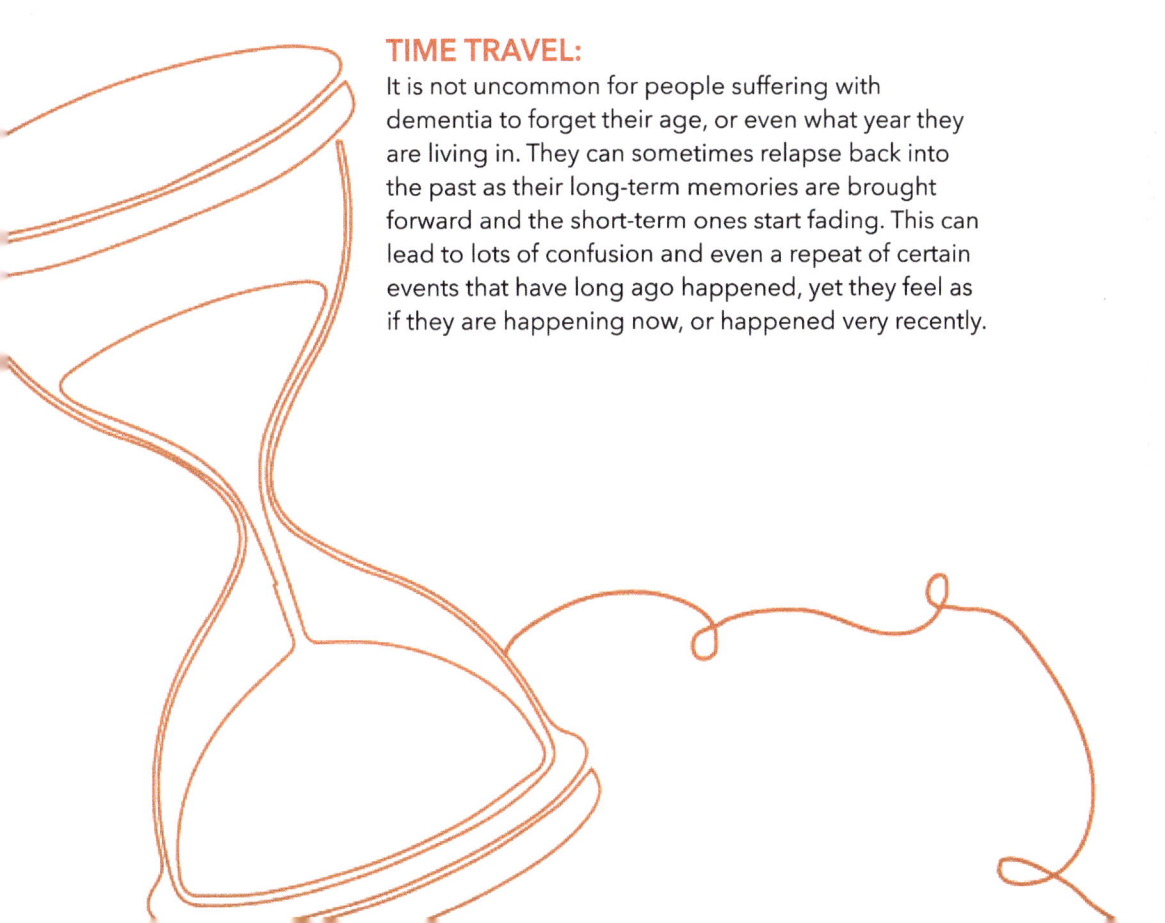

It is not uncommon for people suffering with dementia to forget their age, or even what year they are living in. They can sometimes relapse back into the past as their long-term memories are brought forward and the short-term ones start fading. This can lead to lots of confusion and even a repeat of certain events that have long ago happened, yet they feel as if they are happening now, or happened very recently.

"One night my great uncle gave me some money. He said it was a gift for his night's stay. I told him this was his house, not some hotel, but he kept trying to gift me with money for letting him stay the night!" - Jay

the funny side

Dementia isn't all doom and gloom, some moments are funny and heart-warming and will make you laugh out loud. Dealing with dementia can be a heavy responsibility and sometimes the only way to power through the day is to look for the humour in situations and see the optimism.

Laughing at something funny a dementia patient says or does, doesn't make you a bad person. You're not laughing at them or being mean-spirited, you're laughing at a ridiculous situation. And don't be surprised if they are laughing even louder than you! Humour helps release stress and tension. It also helps you cope with difficult emotions that come up when caring for someone with dementia. Besides, don't you always feel better after a good laugh?

The Funny Side

"MY GRANDMOTHER ONCE TOLD ME THAT IF WE EVER RUN OUT OF DEODORANT, WE CAN ALWAYS USE CUSTARD! IT WAS VERY RANDOM AND SLIGHTLY CONFUSING, BUT FUNNY NEVERTHELESS." – Joe

The Funny Side

People will often say things that make no sense to anyone but themselves; in this case there is no point in disagreeing or correcting, it is best for both parties to just agree. This could be because they have forgotten the meanings of words or just because the connections of what ordinary things are, are lost from their brains, causing them to say very random things.

"My gran once asked for a weapon to be left by her bedside so she could beat off any strangers! She wanted a big stick, we had to talk her out of it for days." – Sophie

DEFENSIVE:
Mistrust of surroundings and people can often lead to defensive behaviour showcased by dementia patients. This isn't always the case, however, a lot of the times defensive behaviour is shown when they fear for their safety. This could be caused by certain hallucinations, forgetting their surroundings, or just a certain mood they wake up in. Dealing with this can be difficult, especially if the person they are mistrusting is you. The best thing to do in a case such as this is to not antagonise them and leave them alone for a while so that they forget about it. If this does not seem to do the trick, then talking to them and reminding them of who you are and that you mean no harm should help.

"My mother-in-law thought there was a rabid dog outside the window barking like crazy. She kept shouting at us and warning us that the dog was going to come and get us all. It was hilarious." - Mack

The Funny Side

Sometimes a trait of dementia is to confuse certain sounds for something else. In the case opposite she may have heard something else such as coughing or laughing and confused it with the sound of an angry dog. Taking sounds and creating scenarios in their mind is not uncommon for patients of this disease, as their memories are all twisted, not allowing them to be able to focus on reality and differentiate between normal sounds and scary sounds.

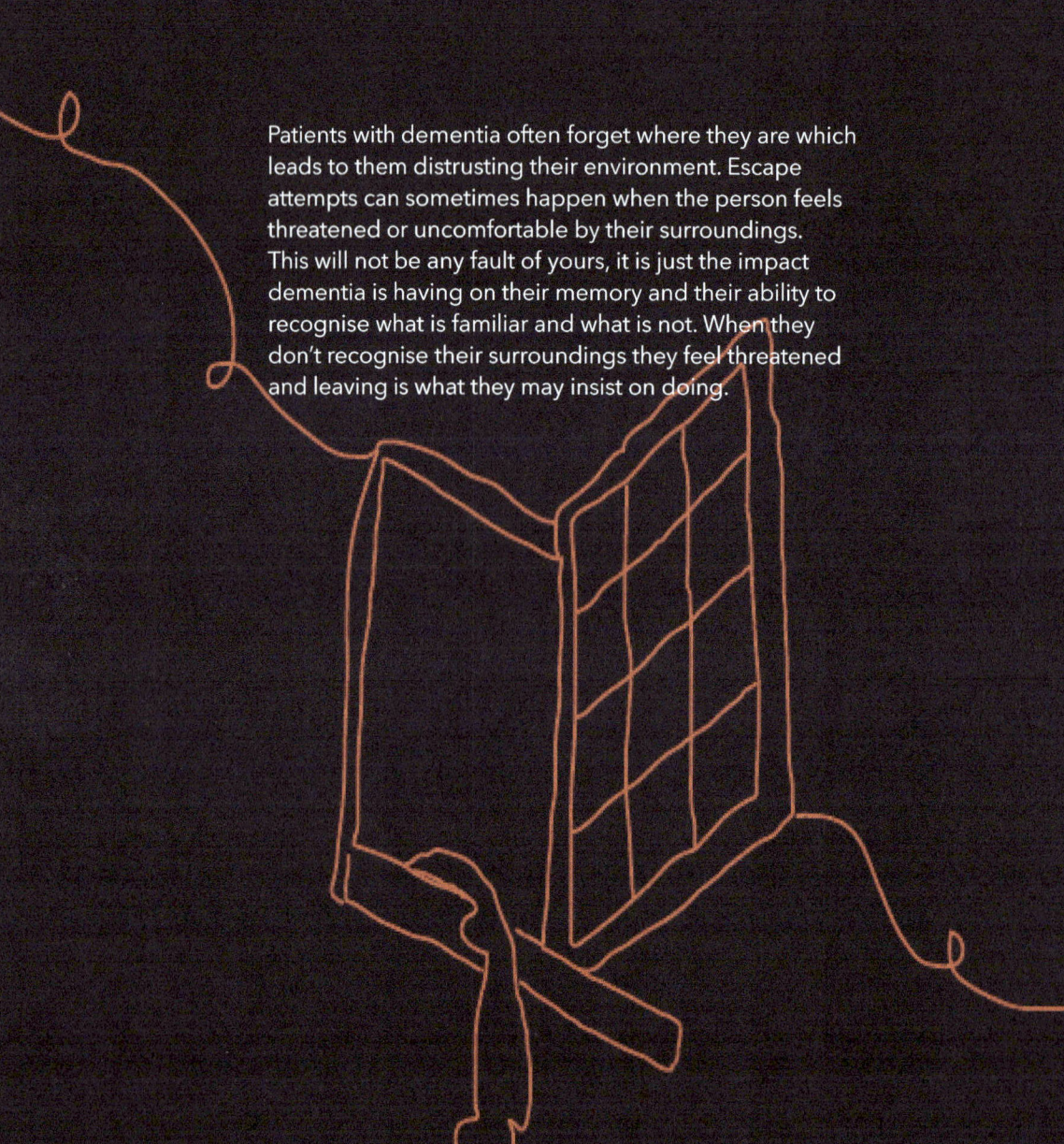

Patients with dementia often forget where they are which leads to them distrusting their environment. Escape attempts can sometimes happen when the person feels threatened or uncomfortable by their surroundings. This will not be any fault of yours, it is just the impact dementia is having on their memory and their ability to recognise what is familiar and what is not. When they don't recognise their surroundings they feel threatened and leaving is what they may insist on doing.

"My great nan with dementia led an escape out of the care home she was in once. I heard they nearly got on the bus and ran away! She managed to convince the others to join her too." – Beth

38 The Funny Side

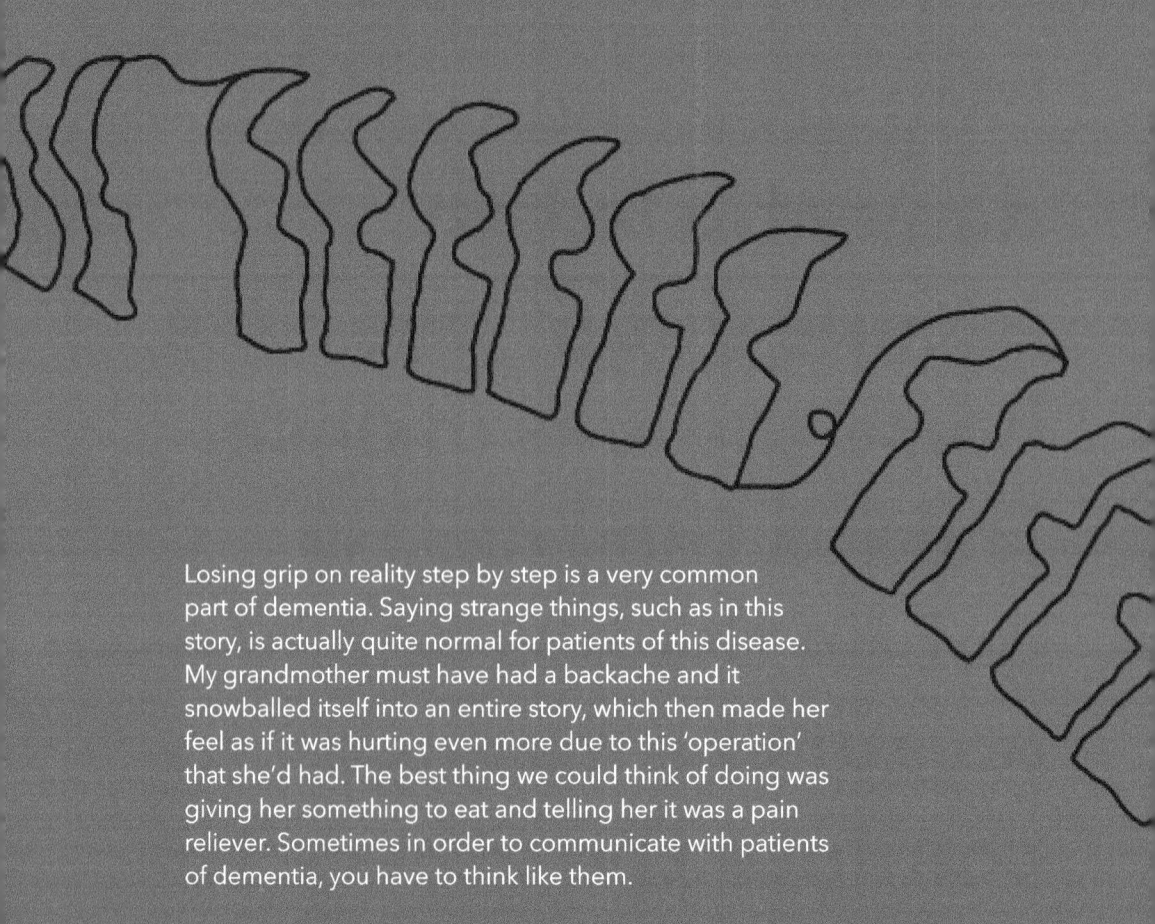

Losing grip on reality step by step is a very common part of dementia. Saying strange things, such as in this story, is actually quite normal for patients of this disease. My grandmother must have had a backache and it snowballed itself into an entire story, which then made her feel as if it was hurting even more due to this 'operation' that she'd had. The best thing we could think of doing was giving her something to eat and telling her it was a pain reliever. Sometimes in order to communicate with patients of dementia, you have to think like them.

"My grandmother was explaining how her back hurt and said, 'You see, one of the clips in my spine has been removed via an operation, so now it hurts more.' She talked about this story for months and told anyone willing to listen." – **Zara**

"My grandparents were on holiday once and my granddad with dementia got confused and went to have a shower in the middle of the night. He ended up locking himself outside and getting yelled at by other holiday goers when he knocked on their doors out of confusion." – **Matt**

WHAT ADVICE

This section of the book aims to leave you with some tips from caregivers and support workers in order to help you as much as possible and make this journey as easy as it can be. Hopefully some of this advice is helpful in dealing with your loved one's condition and making this more bearable for you and them.

PATIENCE:

Dementia is a scary world for the person to live in on its own, but having to live in our world with their ever changing perception of reality and behave accordingly is a big ask. Incidents such as the one mentioned on the opposite page are actually very common for this disease as confusion often leads to mistakes. The best thing to do in this or any situation similar, is to be patient with them. Explain to anyone affected the reason for any disturbances so they can understand better. People with dementia are often met with frustration because people simply do not understand this illness. It is nothing to be embarrassed about as it is not their fault and not in their control.

CALM:

People with dementia often accuse the people closest to them of theft, poisoning, kidnap and other various forms of mistreatment. It's important to keep reminding yourself that this person isn't saying these things on purpose to hurt you. The damage in their brain has caused them to strongly believe things that we know aren't real.

Paranoia and delusions can lead to these accusations and logical answers tend not to work in times such as these. The best course of action is to validate their feelings calmly, and try distracting them and steering them to another topic. If they think food and drink being poisoned, the best thing to do is to show them the food in preparation where possible, or try some of the food from their plate to show them it is safe. Calm and collected responses are the best course of action, no matter how frustrating the situation can get, which it definitely can, so taking a break and time to breathe is extremely important for you and the individual with dementia.

"My mother-in-law thought we were poisoning her food sometimes. I used to try it to show her that it was okay to eat, but this would go back and forth for a while." – Marc

"My grandmother often says she wants to go home even though she is currently at home. She gets so frustrated, sad and sometimes even cries that she just wants to go home home home!" - Zara

Advice **45**

DISTRACTION
Dementia patients often say they want to go home. This does not always have to mean a specific place; it could mean a time or space where they felt happy and secure, so it may not physically exist. They can often become upset, frustrated and even angry; it may even lead to you feeling these things as well, which is nothing to feel guilty about. The best thing to do is to reassure them they are safe here and that they will be okay. Try and distract them and divert the conversation towards something else such as food, music or even a walk.

RECOGNITION

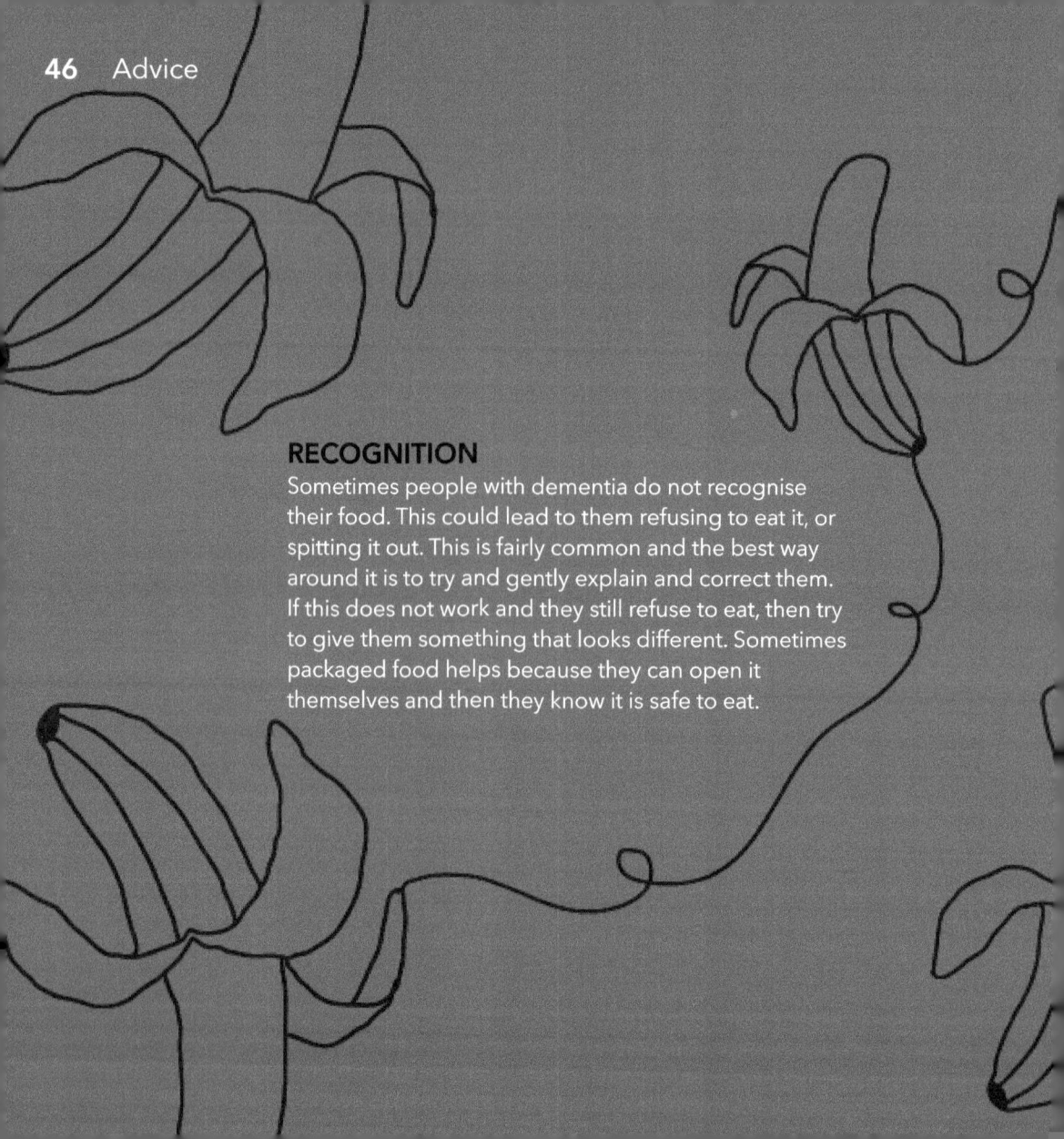

Sometimes people with dementia do not recognise their food. This could lead to them refusing to eat it, or spitting it out. This is fairly common and the best way around it is to try and gently explain and correct them. If this does not work and they still refuse to eat, then try to give them something that looks different. Sometimes packaged food helps because they can open it themselves and then they know it is safe to eat.

"'What is that? It looks like rocks! I'm not eating that.' My gran often refuses to eat her food because she can't recognise it and mistakes it for something else." - Zara

"My mum sometimes thinks I've had an accident when I go out. She gets really worried and upset. She claims she heard it and that I am lying when I say I'm okay." **- Shan**

Advice   **49**

HEARING:
Sometimes hallucinations will come in the form of sounds only; the patient may not see anything, however, they may claim that they hear certain sounds. These can range from positive sounds such as happy voices, to more upsetting sounds such as people being hurt, car accidents, doorbells, etcetera.

Your loved one may become agitated, upset or even angry, depending on the nature of what exactly they are hearing. The best thing to do is to distract them or tell them the sound they heard in fact belongs to something positive. Adding positive connotations to the sounds will make your loved one more at ease and therefore make it easier for everyone.

UNDERSTANDING:

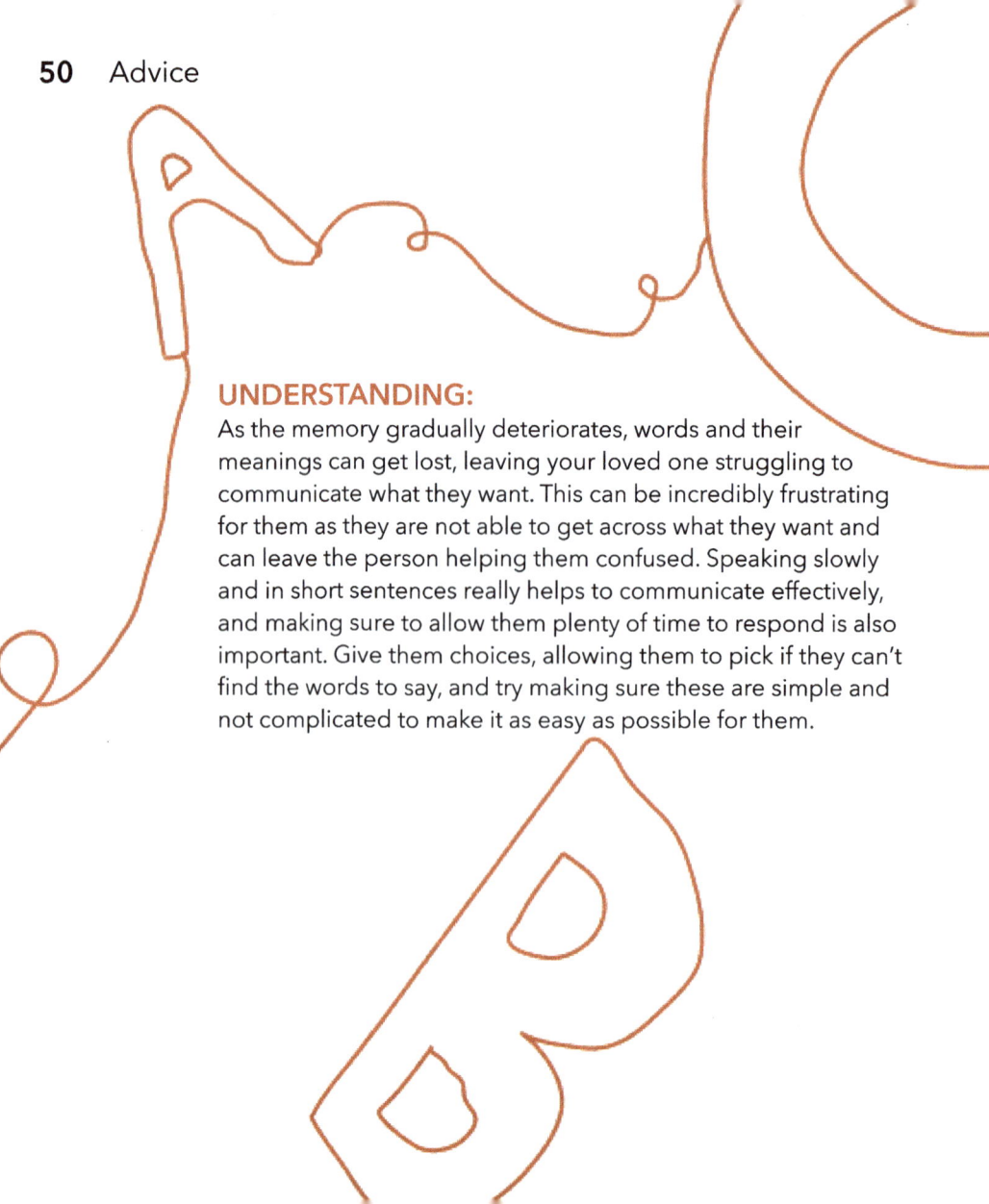

As the memory gradually deteriorates, words and their meanings can get lost, leaving your loved one struggling to communicate what they want. This can be incredibly frustrating for them as they are not able to get across what they want and can leave the person helping them confused. Speaking slowly and in short sentences really helps to communicate effectively, and making sure to allow them plenty of time to respond is also important. Give them choices, allowing them to pick if they can't find the words to say, and try making sure these are simple and not complicated to make it as easy as possible for them.

Advice 51

"Sometimes my wife jumbles her words up so much I have no idea what she's saying! She can say one thing and actually mean the total opposite." – John

"It was ~~weird~~ with my grandad because even though he forgot my name, he would always ask me about my art and stuff, which was nice that he remembered my hobbies and interests." – **Eve**

LUCID MOMENTS

Your loved one may sometimes have lucid moments where they remember certain things perfectly well and it feels as if their dementia has been suddenly cured. This is fairly normal as patients either have certain things that they just don't forget, or they have moments of sudden recollection where they remember small specific details about you, or even themselves. Moments like these are rare and extremely special as it feels as if your loved one is back to their original self for a while. Just enjoy and cherish these heart-warming instances.

Dementia is loud, frustrating, upsetting, amusing, heart-warming and unique to each and every person that it touches. There are moments that are shared by everyone, and some that are individual to just your story.

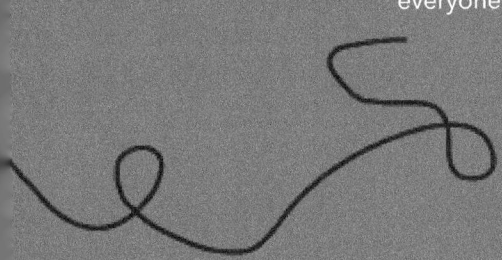

CPSIA information can be obtained
at www.ICGtesting.com
Printed in the USA
BVHW021406060721
611236BV00019B/626